RAYS

▲ S U S A N H . G R A Y

Published in the United States of America by Cherry Lake Publishing
Ann Arbor, Michigan
www.cherrylakepublishing.com

Consultants: Dominique A. Didier, PhD, Associate Professor, Department of Biology, Millersville University;
Marla Conn, ReadAbility, Inc.
Book design: Sleeping Bear Press

Photo Credits: ©StudioSmart/Shutterstock Images, cover, 1; ©Renato Calò/iStockphoto, 5; ©John Mccosh/iStockphoto, 6; ©Richard Bonnett/http://www.flickr.com/CC-BY-2.0, 7; ©Marc Turcan/Shutterstock Images, 9; ©Dorling Kindersley RF/Thinkstock, 11; ©Ethan Daniels/Shutterstock Images, 12; ©Stammers/Dreamstime.com, 15; ©Konoka Amane/Shutterstock Images, 17; ©Ariel Bravy/Shutterstock Images, 18; ©Frankie Grainger/Dreamstime.com, 21; ©Rsazonov/Dreamstime.com, 22; ©Mark Doherty/Dreamstime.com, 23; ©Jung Hsuan/Shutterstock Images, 25; ©THEPALMER/iStockphoto, 26; ©Firststar/Dreamstime.com, 27; ©Circumnavigation/Shutterstock Images, 29

Library of Congress Cataloging-in-Publication Data

Gray, Susan H.
    Rays / by Susan H. Gray.
        pages cm. — (Exploring our oceans)
    Summary: "Discover facts about rays, including physical features, habitat, life cycle, food, and threats to these ocean creatures. Photos, captions, and keywords supplement the narrative of this informational text"— Provided by publisher.
    Audience: 8-12
    Audience: Grade 4 to 6
    Includes bibliographical references and index.
    ISBN 978-1-62431-599-2 (hardcover) — ISBN 978-1-62431-611-1 (pbk.) —
    ISBN 978-1-62431-623-4 (pdf) — ISBN 978-1-62431-635-7 (ebook)
    1. Rays (Fishes)—Juvenile literature. I. Title.

    QL638.8.G73 2014
    597.3'5—dc23   2013031216

Cherry Lake Publishing would like to acknowledge the work of
The Partnership for 21st Century Skills. Please visit *www.p21.org*
for more information.

Printed in the United States of America
Corporate Graphics Inc.
January 2014

ABOUT THE AUTHOR

Susan H. Gray has a master's degree in zoology. She has worked in research and has taught college-level science classes. Susan has also written more than 140 science and reference books, but especially likes to write about animals. She and her husband, Michael, live in Cabot, Arkansas.

TABLE OF CONTENTS

GRACEFUL SWIMMERS

It was a beautiful, clear day, and the sun warmed the ocean. A small group of manta rays swam together through the water. They sailed forward, gracefully flapping their huge fins. Suddenly, one ray shot above the surface and high into the air. It dropped back into the water headfirst. Soon, a second ray did the same thing. A minute or two passed. All of a sudden, a huge manta flew into the air. It flipped over in one great somersault and landed with a splash.

A manta ray leaps from the ocean.

A group of stingrays swims near a reef.

Rays are fish that are related to sharks. Like sharks, they have no bones at all. Instead, their skeletons are made of strong, flexible **cartilage**. Their bodies are flattened, and the fins on their sides are broad and floppy.

The manta ray is just one kind of ray. Stingrays, butterfly rays, electric rays, and sawfish are a few other kinds.

Most rays live in warm, salty seas. They are found in the Pacific, Atlantic, and Indian Oceans. Some rays prefer to swim out in the open water. Others lie quietly on the seafloor.

Only a few **species** live in rivers. These rays are found in South America, western Africa, Southeast Asia, and the United States.

Some scientists suggest this leaping behavior by female rays is related to birthing her pups.

LOOK AGAIN

SCIENTISTS DON'T KNOW WHY SOME RAYS LEAP OUT OF THE WATER. SOME SAY THE RAYS DO THIS TO CLEAN THINGS FROM THEIR BODIES. OTHERS THINK THE RAYS ARE JUST PLAYFUL. WHAT DO YOU THINK?

CHAPTER 2

PANCAKES

Some people say that rays are just sharks that are shaped like pancakes. This is not far from the truth. All rays have flattened bodies. The round stingray, for example, looks like a big pancake with a tail. Another ray, the sawfish, looks more like a shark with a flat belly.

Different groups of rays have different shapes. The main part of a ray's body is called the disc. The disc of the ray is actually formed by the **pectoral** fins, which are attached to the sides of the head. Manta rays and eagle rays have diamond-shaped discs. Butterfly rays have pectoral fins that reach far out to the sides. They look like stretched-out diamonds. Deepwater stingrays have round discs that are pointed in front.

Manta rays are the largest rays. Adults can have "wingspans" of 22 feet (6.7 m) or more. A fully grown manta would easily cover the floor of a two-car garage! The smallest ray known is the short-nose electric ray. It is only 4 inches (10 cm) across. That's smaller than a CD.

Does this look like a pancake with a tail to you?

Eyes are on the upper side of a ray's head. Near each eye is an opening called a spiracle. Spiracles help the ray to breathe. Water moves into them, then across structures in the head called gills. The gills draw oxygen from that water. The oxygen moves from the gills into the blood and then out to the ray's tissues. After the water moves over the gills, it passes out through the gill slits. The gill slits are on the underside of the head.

The mouth of most rays is also on the underside. Some rays have rows and rows of teeth. In certain species, the teeth are fused into rough bands. These form a sort of pavement for grinding food. In other rays, the teeth are pointed. In still others, they are no more than little bumps.

The ray's head bears many special **sensors**. They lie just beneath the skin. The sensors detect electrical fields in the water. Such fields surround fish and other animals. When these animals come near, the ray might not even see them. But its sensors pick them up.

BODY DIAGRAM

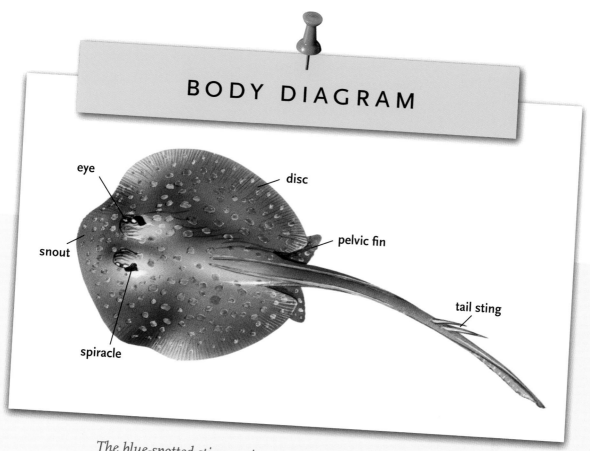

eye

disc

snout

pelvic fin

spiracle

tail sting

The blue-spotted stingray is a small- to medium-sized stingray.

The electric ray has additional organs on its head. These are the electric organs called **electroplaques**. They appear as two big lumps just under the skin. They can produce quite an electric shock. The jolt is enough to knock a predator backward. It can totally stun small prey animals. In some species the charge is enough to knock a grown man unconscious.

Can you determine what type of rays these are?

Large pectoral fins flare out from each side of the ray's body and attach to the sides of the head. The fins are thin and floppy and give the ray its shape. Some rays swim by flapping these like wings. Others swim by rippling their pectoral fins.

Many rays are dull gray, brown, or blue, with light-colored bellies. But some rays have beautiful colors and patterns. Spotted eagle rays have dark skin covered with whitish dots and circles. The bullseye electric ray has a single large "target" on its back. And blue-spotted rays are covered with bright blue spots.

The skin on the back might be smooth or rough. Some rays are covered with tiny, overlapping toothlike scales. They make the skin feel like sandpaper. Certain stingrays also bear larger, pointed structures called thorns.

Some rays, such as the butterfly rays, have short, stubby tails. Others, like the eagle rays, have tails that are long and slender. Many rays have sharp spines on their tails. In stingrays and round rays, these spines may be quite **venomous**. Rays with such spines will thrust them into any animal that threatens them. The spines are jagged, with backward-pointing barbs.

THINK ABOUT IT

WHEN PEOPLE ARE STUNG BY RAYS, THE SPINE OFTEN BECOMES STUCK IN THEIR SKIN. DOCTORS WARN THEM NOT TO PULL IT OUT. WHY WOULD THEY SAY THIS?

YUM!

Rays eat all sorts of small **aquatic** animals. But different rays eat different things. It all depends on where they live, their behavior, and how their bodies are built.

Many stingrays live in shallow areas, partly buried in the sand. Because the mouth is on the underside, rays eat a lot of bottom-dwelling animals. These include worms, lobsters, and crabs. Some stingrays swim the open sea. They catch small fish, squid, shrimp, and jellyfish.

The round rays also lie on the seafloor, often among rocks and plants. They flap their fins to disturb the sand and unearth their food. They feed on small fish, worms, shrimp, and other small prey.

A curious fish comes upon a ray hiding in the sand.

The Pacific electric ray is another fish that inhabits the sandy bottom. During the day, it rests, buried and hidden from view. When a fish comes near, the ray stuns it with an electrical shock. Then it wraps its disc around the prey. Finally, it maneuvers the fish around to be swallowed headfirst. In dark or murky water, this ray moves along just above the seafloor. It senses the electrical fields of its prey. It stuns and eats any small fish unlucky enough to come near.

Eagle rays and cownose rays swim along close to the sandy bottom. They fan their pectoral fins to disturb the sand and expose small prey. With their shovel-shaped snouts, they scoop up clams, oysters, and other **mollusks**. The teeth of these rays are made up of **interlocking** plates. They crush and grind the shells and spit them out. They swallow the soft animals left behind.

The mouth and gill slits are on the underside of a stingray.

LOOK AGAIN

DO YOU SEE A FACE HERE? THE SPOTS NEAR THE CORNERS OF THE MOUTH ARE NOT EYES. THEY ARE SIMILAR TO NOSTRILS AND ALLOW THE RAY TO SMELL.

Some species of sawfish can grow to a length of 25 feet (7.6 m).

The manta ray is an open-water swimmer. It has small fins that looks like horns on either side of its mouth. This ray's huge mouth is at the very front edge of its disc. Therefore, the manta is not built for bottom-feeding. Instead, it swims through the ocean with its mouth wide open. The little fins position themselves to form a funnel. As the ray moves forward, water funnels into its mouth. Strainers deep in the throat catch small fish and **plankton**.

The sawfish is one of the most unusual rays. It is not as flat as its cousins. It has a long snout, or saw, with sharp, pointy teeth around the edge. It also has an excellent system for detecting electrical fields.

The sawfish lives along coastlines, in **estuaries**, and in rivers. In these places, the water is often muddy. The sawfish cannot use its vision to hunt. But a prey animal's electrical field alerts the sawfish that food is nearby. This throws the sawfish into action. With one jerk of the head, it can slice a fish in two.

CHAPTER 4

BABY RAYS

Every year or two, male and female rays come together to mate. At this time, the males deposit **sperm** cells in the bodies of the females. These cells unite with egg cells in the female, and tiny rays begin to form. They grow and develop inside a special chamber in the mother's body.

At first, each growing embryo gets its food from a yolk sac. The sac is attached to its little body. When the yolk is gone, the baby feeds on a rich, milky fluid produced by the mother. It is loaded with fat and protein. The tiny rays continue to grow and develop inside their mother until it's time for their birth. The length of this growth period is different for different species. Many ray species need only three months to develop. But the largetooth sawfish takes five months. Some stingrays take as long as 12 months.

In the wild, stingrays can live to be 15 to 25 years old.

Blue-spotted rays often swim near coral reefs.

LOOK AGAIN

WHEN THEY'RE BORN, BABY RAYS ALREADY KNOW HOW TO SWIM. HOW MIGHT THIS PROTECT THEM?

At some time before birth, baby stingrays develop a temporary covering over their spines. Baby sawfish grow a similar covering over their saws. This protects the mother during birth. It also keeps the baby sawfish from hurting their brothers and sisters.

Just before they are born, the babies roll up like burritos. Then they slide away from their mother and into the sea. Right away, they unfurl their pectoral fins and begin to swim.

The babies look just like miniature adults. At birth, they can already fend for themselves. They do not need the care of their parents.

Different species of rays have different numbers of babies. The mantas are at the low end. They usually have only one pup, but what a baby it is! It may be more than 4 feet (1.2 m) across and weigh more than 20 pounds (9.1 kg)!

At the other end of the scale are the Pacific electric rays and the sawfish. Pacific electric rays have up to 20 babies, all around 8 inches (20 cm) long. In their first year, these little fish can more than double in length. The smalltooth sawfish also has up to 20 young. These babies are about 2.5 feet (0.8 m) long.

Most electric rays live in shallow water and are harmless unless touched or stepped on.

CHAPTER 5

RAYS IN TROUBLE

The populations of many rays are shrinking. It's hard to imagine that rays might be disappearing. After all, they can protect themselves from most predators. They can sting or electrocute their enemies. Sawfish can slash other animals to pieces. Some rays avoid danger simply by hiding. And mantas are just too huge to attack. So what are the problems that rays are facing?

Some rays do become victims of predators, mainly sharks. Scientists have found sharks with ray spines stuck in their mouths and lips. This shows that sharks and rays sometimes tangle. Hammerhead sharks are known to whack stingrays with their heads. Then they press the rays to the seafloor and proceed to eat them.

Covered almost entirely in sand, this blue-spotted ray is barely visible.

Fishing boats searching for tuna can accidentally catch rays.

Predators are not the biggest problem, though. Rays are threatened in other ways. Some people fish for rays. But often, rays get caught in nets or lines meant to trap other fish. Sawfish are especially likely to become entangled.

Most people do not care for ray meat. So those who fish for rays usually sell their other body parts. Fins are sometimes sold to make shark fin soup. Liver oil is often used in Chinese medicine. Parts of manta gills go to buyers across Asia. Saws are sold to tourists.

Sold in dry fish markets of southern China, dried rays are sometimes cooked into a broth used as medicine.

Changes in the rays' **habitats** can also cause problems. South America's freshwater stingrays cannot withstand changes in the environment. They need very specific amounts of oxygen, salt, and acid in their water. Sometimes wastes from fields, towns, or factories run into their rivers. These can change the makeup of the water and kill the rays.

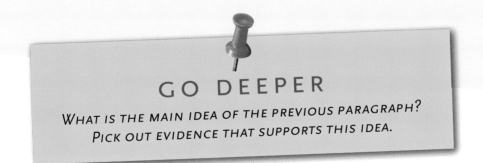

GO DEEPER

WHAT IS THE MAIN IDEA OF THE PREVIOUS PARAGRAPH? PICK OUT EVIDENCE THAT SUPPORTS THIS IDEA.

What if all the threats were removed? The ray populations would still take a long time to recover. This is because of the rays' own nature. It takes many years for a ray to grow old enough to have babies. Some rays have only one or two pups at a time. At best, rays will give birth only once a year. And many mothers need two years or more between births.

Fortunately, experts worldwide are working to protect rays. Laws are in place to stop habitat destruction. The International Union for Conservation of Nature (IUCN) classifies five species of sawfish as **Endangered** on its Red List of Threatened Species. This means that populations have a very high risk of becoming **extinct**. Scientists in many countries noticed that manta fishing was on the rise. The IUCN is working to protect this ray.

Certainly rays need more protection. These graceful animals will hopefully be around for years to come.

More than 1,000 manta rays are caught per year in some areas. Their large size and slow swimming speed make them an easy target.

THINK ABOUT IT

- In chapter 2, we learned that rays come in many colors. Some rays like to hide out in the sand and mud on the seafloor. What colors do you think those rays are?

- What was the most surprising thing you learned about rays?

- Chapter 3 told how eagle rays eat clams and oysters. But these rays also destroy oyster beds grown by farmers. How could oyster farmers protect their beds without harming the rays?

- In chapter 5, we saw that fishing can threaten ray populations. Some rays are caught and sent to public aquariums. There, people admire the rays and come to respect them. But those rays were taken from their natural homes. So, is it good for these rays to go to aquariums or not?

LEARN MORE

FURTHER READING

Parker, Steve. *Fish*. New York: DK Children, 2005.

Sjonger, Rebecca, and Bobbie Kalman. *Skates and Rays*. New York: Crabtree Publishing, 2005.

Spelman, Lucy. *National Geographic Animal Encyclopedia: 2,500 Animals with Photos, Maps, and More!* Washington, DC: National Geographic Children's Books, 2012.

WEB SITES

The Elasmodiver Shark and Ray Field Guide
www.elasmodiver.com/sharks_and_rays.html
This page is full of photos and general facts about sharks and rays.

Enchanted Learning—All About Sharks: Manta Ray
www.enchantedlearning.com/subjects/sharks/rays/Mantaray.shtml
Read basic information on the manta ray.

Ichthyology at the Florida Museum of Natural History—Ray and Skate Basics
www.flmnh.ufl.edu/fish/education/questions/raybasics.html
The most commonly asked questions about rays and skates are answered at this site.

National Geographic Kids—Stingrays
http://kids.nationalgeographic.com/kids/animals/creaturefeature/stingray/
Find lots of information about stingrays.

GLOSSARY

aquatic (uh-KWAH-tik) relating to water, or living in water

cartilage (KAHR-tuh-lij) a tough, flexible animal tissue that is whitish or yellowish in color

electroplaques (ih-LEK-truh-plaks) thick tissues in the disc of electric rays that emit electricity

endangered (en-DAYN-jurd) at risk of becoming extinct or of dying out

estuaries (ES-choo-er-eez) the mouths of rivers where they open out into the sea

extinct (ik-STINGKT) no longer found alive

habitats (HAB-ih-tats) the places where animals or plants naturally live

interlocking (in-tur-LOK-eng) connected in such a way as to be locked together

mollusks (MAH-luhsks) soft-bodied animals that have no backbones and are often enclosed in shells

pectoral (PEK-tur-ul) on, near to, or relating to the chest

plankton (PLANGK-tuhn) aquatic plants and animals that are usually small and that drift in the water

sensors (SEN-sawrs) things that can detect and measure changes and transmit that information

species (SPEE-sheez) one type, or kind, of plant or animal

sperm (SPURM) male reproductive cell

venomous (VEN-uhm-uss) having the ability to inflict a poisonous wound

INDEX

DATE DUE

			PRINTED IN U.S.A.